BIBLE
INF●GRAPHICS
FOR KIDS

VOLUME 2

HARVEST kids

HARVEST HOUSE PUBLISHERS
Eugene, Oregon

CREATED BY

HARVEST HOUSE BIBLE INFOGRAPHICS TEAM

Illustrations by **BRIAN HURST**

HEATHER GREEN

AARON DILLON

KYLE HATFIELD

NICOLE DOUGHERTY

KYLER DOUGHERTY

BOOK COVER DESIGN

SPECIAL THANKS ➤ **SARAH GILL** **KEN CARSON** **GENE SKINNER** **DEREK DOUGHERTY**

Library of Congress Cataloging-in-Publication Data

Names: Harvest House Publishers.
Title: Bible infographics for kids.
Description: Eugene, Oregon : Harvest House Publishers, 2018. | Includes bibliographical references.
Identifiers: LCCN 2017028151 (print) | LCCN 2017034594 (ebook) | ISBN 9780736972437 (ebook) | ISBN 9780736972420 (hardcover)
Subjects: LCSH: Bible—Criticism, interpretation, etc.—Juvenile literature. | Bible—Miscellanea.
Classification: LCC BS539 (ebook) | LCC BS539 .B53 2018 (print) | DDC 220.6/1—dc23

LC record available at https://lccn.loc.gov/2017028151

Bible Infographics for Kids Vol. 2
Copyright © 2019 by Harvest House Publishers
Published by Harvest House Publishers
Eugene, Oregon 97408
www.harvesthousepublishers.com
ISBN 978-0-7369-7632-9 (hardcover)

Printed in China
19 20 21 22 23 24 25 26 27 / RDS / 10 9 8 7 6 5 4 3 2 1

It's epic. It's world changing. It's a DICHOTOMY!

Wait...It's a what-*omy*? Well, that's a fancy way of saying opposites.

And this book is full of AMAZING OPPOSITES

Dig in and learn how these important, eye-popping opposites show how
God is THE light and overcomes the darkness no matter what form it takes.

Still confused about INFOGRAPHICS?

Just know that **INFOGRAPHICS HELP YOU SEE INFORMATION**
using a combination of fun facts and craze-mazing visuals.

NOW we're ready.   LET'S GO!

CONTENTS

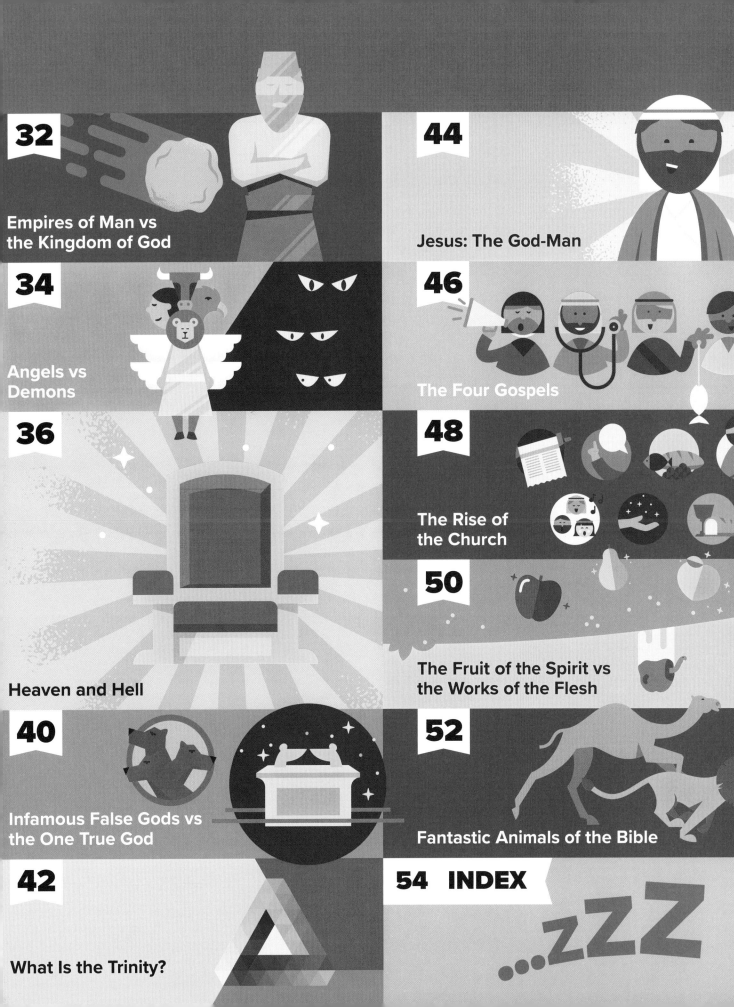

GOD IS LIGHT

"The LORD is my light and my salvation—
whom shall I fear? The LORD is the stronghold
of my life—of whom shall I be afraid?"

Psalm 27:1

JESUS IS LIGHT

"I am the light of the world. Whoever
follows me will never walk in darkness,
but will have the light of life."

John 8:12

THE WORD IS LIGHT

"Your word is a lamp for my
feet, a light on my path."

Psalm 119:105

GOD'S LIGHT
PROTECTS

Psalm 27:1

GOD'S LIGHT EXPOSES
THE DARKNESS

Ephesians 5:11-13

GOD'S CHILDREN
WALK IN THE LIGHT

1 Thessalonians 5:5

LIGHT & DARKNESS IN THE BIBLE
GOD BRINGS LIGHT INTO THE DARKNESS

DARKNESS REPRESENTS
UNKNOWING

Psalm 82:5

DARKNESS REPRESENTS
FOOLISHNESS

Ecclesiastes 2:14

DARKNESS REPRESENTS
PUNISHMENT

Lamentations 3:2

DARKNESS CASTS A SHADOW
(DOUBT) ON THE LIGHT (TRUTH)

Genesis 3:1

DARKNESS MAKES US
WANT TO HIDE

Genesis 3:10

DARKNESS
REPRESENTS EVIL

Proverbs 2:13-14

FACTS ABOUT LIGHT

1. Where light exists, **there is no darkness.**

2. **Light is eternal**—there's nothing else (in the physical world) like it.

3. **Light is mostly invisible**—we only see a small portion, which is what we call **COLOR.**

4. **Light travels at a speed of**
   670,616,629 MPH.

Light would circle the earth **7.5 times** in one second!

 Can YOU spin in a circle 7.5 times in one second?

5. **Light is measured in light-years,** which is the distance light travels in one year:
   5,878,625,000,000 MILES.

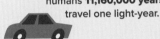 Traveling at 60 MPH, it would take humans **11,160,000 years** to travel one light-year.

SPEED LIMIT 60

Our sun is **.00001581 light-years** from earth, so the light we see from it is
8 min and 20 sec old

The closest star to our galaxy is **4.2 light-years away,** so the light we see is
4.2 years old

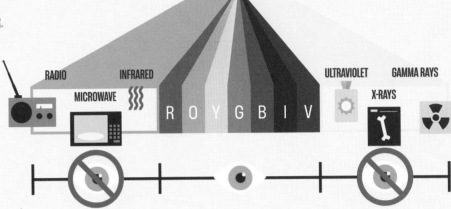

RADIO MICROWAVE INFRARED ROYGBIV ULTRAVIOLET X-RAYS GAMMA RAYS

! God, like light, is so much more than what we can see! **We only see a fraction of what God is up to at any moment.**

! Our universe is so huge that the stars we see in the night sky are actually just the light finally reaching our eyes after traveling various light-years at the speed of light. **So we're actually seeing what the stars looked like in the past!**

FACTS ABOUT DARKNESS

1. **Shadows** (darkness) happen when something blocks the light.

2. Darkness is literally the **absence of light.**

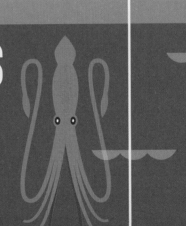

3,280'
The Point of Total Darkness

36,200'
The Mariana Trench

39,000'

 THE DEEPEST SPOT IN THE OCEAN is the **Mariana Trench** in the Pacific Ocean. That's almost as deep as how high airplanes fly!

EGYPT MOSES

VS

Adopted and raised in the Pharaoh's palace—he enjoyed the princely life. A big fan of justice and fairness, this impetuous youth **sometimes handled things the wrong way.** Murder is wrong, kids.

Age(s): 3 months–40 years
Spouse(s): 0 (Many Egyptian men had several!)
Children: 0

Education: Well-educated
Occupation: Prince
Religion: Hebrew
Character: Proud & brave

Likes: His Hebrew people
Dislikes: His people being mistreated
Wanted for: Murder!

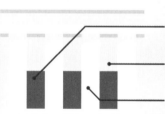

- An indoor pool!
- Many rooms
- Columned halls

- Wig on a bald head
- Used a type of toothbrush
- Clean-shaven
- Used deodorant
- Shirtless
- No underwear
- Kilt
- White linen

FIRST 40 YEARS

Moses is born
Exodus 2:1-4

Pharaoh's daughter adopts Moses
Exodus 2:5-10

Learns about God (from mom) and ruling Egypt (from Pharaoh)

Kills an Egyptian
Exodus 2:11-14

Times Moses is mentioned by name = 10

WILDERNESS MOSES

A poor shepherd, on the run for murder.
He was humbled and ready to free his people.
God uses the humble!

Age(s): 40 years–80 years	**Education:** School of hard knocks	**Likes:** Humility, Israel	
Spouse(s): 1 (Zipporah)	**Occupation:** Midianite herdsman	**Dislikes:** Public speaking	
Children: 2 (Gershom and Eleazer)	**Religion:** Kenite/Israelite	**Abilities:** Talking to burning bushes	
	Character: Humble & bold		

- Older
- Bearded
- Cloak
- Wool
- Linen
- Underwear
- Tunics
- Shoes

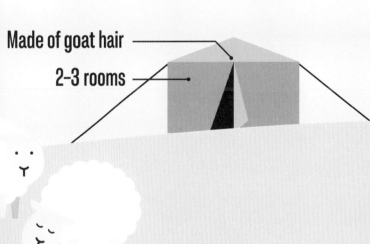

- Made of goat hair
- 2-3 rooms

SECOND 40 YEARS

Runs away to Midian
Exodus 2:15

Gets married and has two sons
Exodus 2:16-22

Works as shepherd for Jethro for 40 years!
Acts 7:30

Talks to a burning bush
Exodus 3

Receives signs from God
Exodus 4:1-17

Returns to Egypt
Exodus 4:18-31

767 Times in the Old Testament

79 Times in the New Testament

HEROES

ESTHER
The Brave Queen

Smartly **earned the king's trust** and used that favor to save her people!

JOSEPH
The Shepherd Dreamer

Patriarch of the Israelites, dream interpreter, and lover of fancy coats. **Saved Egypt and his family from starvation.**

DEBORAH
The Prophetess

The one and only female judge! A wise, courageous, and bold heroine.

PAUL
The Last Apostle

Dramatically converted Pharisee and persecutor of Christians. **Wrote 13 books of the Bible in his spare time.**

JESUS'S RELATIVE

RAHAB
The Unexpected Hero

Bravely hid spies sent into Jericho. Outsmarted the king, knowing God would give the Israelites victory.

NOAH'S RELATIVE

ABRAHAM
The Father of Many

First man chosen by God for a role in the plan of redemption (Genesis 14).

ENOCH
The Guy Who Didn't Die

METHUSELEH'S FATHER

Taken straight to heaven after 365 years on earth.

JOHN THE BAPTIST
The First Baptist

JESUS'S COUSIN

The Nazarite precursor to Jesus. Beheaded by order of Herod (and the scheming of Herodias).

SAMUEL
The Second Moses

Anointed Saul and David. Prophet, priest, and last of the 15 judges mentioned in the book of Judges.

PRISCILLA & AQUILA
The Married Missionaries

Husband and wife refugees working as tentmakers who met Paul and **risked their lives to save his.**

STEPHEN
The Martyr

The first great apologist for Christianity and "a man full of faith and the Holy Spirit" (Acts 6:3).

SILAS
The Scribe

Well-educated prophet and, likely, Roman citizen. **A real smarty-pants.**

FIND THESE HIDDEN OBJECTS

Ruler

Hammer

Pair of Scissors

3 Pencils

Cell Phone

Guitar

4 Carots

Loaf of Bread

3 Red Tomatoes

Gooey Cheeseburger

Popsicle

Pepperoni Pizza

2 Stacks of Coins

2 Stacks of Bills

Sparkly Gold Brick

Shiny Pearl

Bag of Money

Award Ribbon

VILLAINS

CAIN
The First Murderer

The first kid ever and first person labeled unrighteous. Killed his brother Abel and was kicked out of Eden.

JUDAS ISCARIOT
The Traitor

Betrayed Jesus. He felt so guilty for what he'd done, he sadly hanged himself.

LUCIFER/ SATAN
The Devil

Deceiver, tempter, liar, and accuser. The serpent in the garden, chief of the fallen angels, and rebel against God...but still under God's authority. Already defeated and will be judged at the end!

SAUL
The Persecutor

Greek-educated Roman citizen, **totally committed to persecuting Christians.** Met Jesus and experienced a life-changing transformation.

JEZEBEL
The Heartless Queen

Insisted on worshipping Baal and led a campaign to exterminate all the prophets of God.

PONTIUS PILATE
The Convicter

A Roman prefect who persecuted Jews. **Responsible for convicting Jesus.**

HEROD THE GREAT
The Cruel Ruler

Murdered several members of his own family. When told of Jesus's birth, he ordered all male children in the region under age 2 to be killed.

HERODIAS
The Head Huntress

Was married to Philip but divorced him to marry Herod Antipas. **Orchestrated John the Baptist's death** after he strongly and publicly denounced her marriage to Herod.

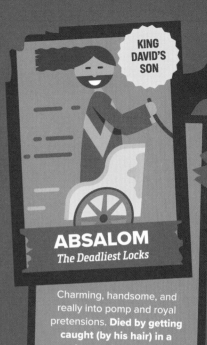

KING DAVID'S SON

ABSALOM
The Deadliest Locks

Charming, handsome, and really into pomp and royal pretensions. **Died by getting caught (by his hair) in a tree and stabbed.**

DELILAH
The Traitorous Hairdresser

Cunning as they come, she was **motivated by greed to subdue Samson.**

HAMAN
The Hater

Deceitful and vengeful Persian noble and high official under King Xerxes. After Mordecai refused to bow to him, he angrily **decided to hate Mordecai and ALL of his people too.**

GOLIATH
The Warrior Giant

A well-armored and strong Philistine champion. Defeated by a shepherd boy wielding a slingshot and a stone, but **ultimately his own sword killed him.**

FEATS OF GOD

FEATS HAPPEN WHEN PEOPLE TRUST GOD.

FAILURES OF MEN

FAILURES HAPPEN WHEN PEOPLE ARE DISOBEDIENT OR SIN.

WITH MAN THIS IS IMPOSSIBLE, BUT WITH GOD ALL THINGS ARE POSSIBLE.

Matthew 19:26

Outran a Chariot
1 Kings 18:46

After a confrontation with the prophets of Baal on Mt. Carmel, Elijah ran to Jezreel in the power of the Lord. **He outran Ahab, who was riding in a chariot.**

Turtle
4 mph

Average 12-year-old boy
6-7 mph

Usain Bolt (world's fastest man)
28 mph

Chariot
35-40 mph

Married the Wrong Gal
Genesis 29:14-27

Jacob fell in love with Rachel. Rachel's father, Laban, said Jacob could marry her after working for him for 7 years. After the 7 years, **he was tricked into marrying Rachel's sister instead.** Oops!

I do!?

Strong Man
Judges 16:3

To avoid capture, Samson took the city gates (including their two posts) from Gaza and **carried them 1/4 mile** to the hill facing Hebron.

5 TONS

Tragic Haircut
Judges 16:4-22

Samson fell in love with Delilah. But the Philistines wanted her to find out the secret to Samson's strength. Once she learned the secret, she had his head shaved, **his strength was gone, and he was captured.**

Bringing Down the House
Judges 16:23-31

After Delilah's betrayal, Samson was used by the Philistines to celebrate a false god, Dagon. **Samson prayed to God for his strength to return**, and when he pushed on the two support pillars, the temple collapsed.

Walked on Water...at First

Matthew 14:22-33

While on a boat, the disciples saw Jesus walking on the water. At Jesus's word, Peter **got out of the boat and walked on the water too** until he became afraid—**then he began to sink.**

Some animals, like the Basilisk lizard, **can run on water.**

Denied!

Luke 22:54-62

At the Last Supper, Jesus predicted that Peter would deny Him. Peter was sure that he would never do that to Jesus. **He ended up denying Jesus not once but three times.**

NOPE.

NOT ME.

NO WAY!

A Bold Preacher

Acts 2:14-41

Peter went from being all talk about not denying Jesus (but then actually denying Him) to using his words to preach boldly. **3,000 people were saved.**

Teleported

Acts 8:26-40

An angel told Philip to go to Gaza. Following the Holy Spirit's direction, Philip talked to an Ethiopian man who was reading the book of Isaiah. Right after witnessing to and baptizing the man, **Philip was miraculously transported about 20 miles away** to Azotus.

Azotus
20mi
Gaza

Didn't Die

Genesis 5:21-24

Enoch was such good friends with God that God didn't make him experience death. **He was simply taken up into heaven.**

Elijah was also taken into heaven **without dying.**

Reluctant Prophet

Jonah 1:3, 4:1-11

God told Jonah to preach to Nineveh, but **Jonah boarded a boat to run away and ended up being swallowed by a big fish.** After 3 days, the fish spit him up.

BIBLICAL LANDMARKS

Greater Ararat: **16,854'**

Lesser Ararat: **12,782'**

Matterhorn: **14,692'**

Mt. Fuji: **12,389'**

MT. ARARAT

Last erupted in 1840

Resting place of **Noah's Ark** after the flood
Genesis 8

MT. SINAI

Symbolizes God's covenant and His presence

Moses recieves the **10 commandments**
Exodus 20; 34

Mt. Sinai: **7,497'**

TWO WAYS TO GO UP!

1. Climb 3,750 steps
(That's about 2.3 Empire State Buildings)

2. Ride a camel

Going up?

SEA LEVEL

RED SEA

Originally: **Reed Sea**

Mistranslated to: **Red Sea**

Where the Israelites miraculously walked through on dry land.
Exodus 14

Where the Israelites crossed the sea, it would have taken them **about 4 hours**, and it would have taken the waters only **half an hour** to go back to normal.

1,450 miles long

7,254' below sea level

180 miles wide (average)

WHERE THERE'S WIND, THERE'S A WAY
Scientists found that wind blowing 67 mph overnight **could expose land under water.**

DEAD SEA

Symbolizes life apart from the law of God

Sodom and Gomorrah
Genesis 19

David's hiding place from Saul
1 Samuel 23–24

SALTY!
This sea has some of the saltiest water on earth because the water has no way to escape except by evaporating. With **temperatures that can reach 130° F,** water evaporates quickly!

WORLD'S LOWEST-ELEVATION LAKE

1300' below sea level
(2400' at its deepest point)

Ancient Dead Sea | Current Dead Sea

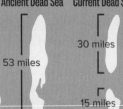

53 miles | 30 miles

10 miles | 15 miles

Salty water makes it easy to float and is great for skin conditions!
The Dead Sea was home to the first "health resort" for Herod the Great.

Dead Sea : **34.2%**

Ocean: **3.5%**

MT. MORIAH

Also called Temple Mount

Where God provided a ram
for Abraham to sacrifice
instead of Isaac.
Genesis 22

Home of Solomon's Temple
2 Chronicles 3

MT. OF OLIVES

Symbolizes Israel, the presence
of God, sanctification, and the
renewal of God's kingdom

Where Jesus taught
Mark 13

Where Jesus was arrested
Mark 14

MT. ZION

Symbolizes God's dwelling
place and is a shadow of the
heavenly reality. God is with us,
unconquerable, and unshakable.

The name of one of the
fortresses David captured
when conquering Jerusalem

MENTIONED 152 TIMES IN THE OLD TESTAMENT

6 times
literal "Mt. Zion"

53 times
in poetry

93 times
in prophetic
literature

GOLGOTHA

Symbolizes where sin was
conquered once and for all

Where Jesus was crucified
Matthew 27:32-56

Mt of Olives: **2,500'**

Mt Moriah: **2428'**

Jerusalem: **2,474'**

Mt Zion: **2,510'**

JORDAN RIVER

Symbolizes freedom and
entering into God's promises

📍 The Israelites crossed the river into
the Promised Land **on dry land.**
Joshua 3:14-17

📍 **Elijah went up to heaven** in a
whirlwind after crossing the river
on dry ground with Elisha.
2 Kings 2:6-12

📍 **Where Jesus was baptized**
Matthew 4:13-17

PROMISED LAND

MAKE WAY!
There is evidence that when the
Israelites crossed over the river, a
landslide temporarily stopped the
water. How cool that God could
cause a landslide at **exactly the
right moment** to allow the
priests to cross the river!

🏆 **WORLD'S LOWEST-ELEVATION RIVER**

Sea of
Galilee

STARTS
7' above
sea level

165 miles of
winding river,
85 miles long.
2'-10' deep
and 100' wide
(average)

ENDS
1274' below
sea level

Dead
Sea

GETHSEMANE

Symbolizes where Jesus suffered;
a "dark night of the soul"

📍 **Where Jesus prayed**
before His crucifixion
Matthew 26:36-44

📍 **Where Judas betrayed Jesus**
Luke 22:1-6, 47-48

Olive Tree
926 years old

Grand Abuelo,
Andes
3646 years old

Methuselah,
California
4848 years old

LONG LIVE OLIVE TREES!
Some trees date back to AD 1092, though they
could be older because olive trees can grow
back from roots even after being cut down.
**Therefore, they could have been the same
trees Jesus wept under** in Luke 22:43-44!

THE ROMAN COLOSSEUM

AD 70/80 · Rome, Italy

Housed the bloody games where gladiators, criminals (including Christians), and even animals would fight to the death.

157' tall

RUINS

! It could hold about **50,000 spectators,** which is almost the same as Yankee Stadium (52,325).

THE PARTHENON

436 BC · Athens, Greece

It replaced an existing temple destroyed by the Persian empire and was dedicated to Athena.

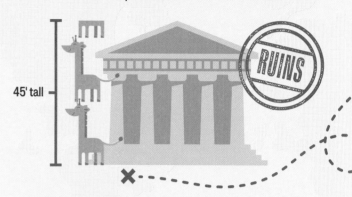

45' tall

RUINS

! **Advanced architecture:** The columns all lean inward slightly to create the illusion of straight lines.

WONDERS ·+OF· THE

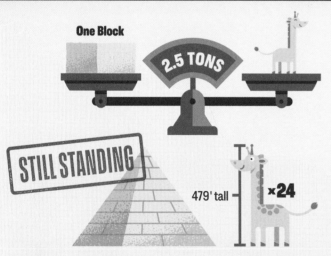

One Block

2.5 TONS

STILL STANDING

479' tall ×24

! The temperature inside of the pyramid **never changes from 68° F.** This is also the earth's average temperature.

THE GREAT PYRAMID OF GIZA

c. 2600 BC · El Giza, Egypt

It was built to guide ships into its busy harbor. Rumors say it may have also been used to light enemy ships on fire.

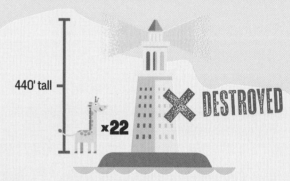

440' tall ×22 DESTROYED

! **The first lighthouse**—it used mirrors to reflect sunlight and could be seen up to 35 miles out to sea.

THE LIGHTHOUSE OF ALEXANDRIA

3rd century BC · Island of Pharos, Egypt

SOLOMON'S TEMPLE

 c. 970 BC   Jerusalem

1 Kings 6

This temple was the most important center of religion for the Israelites for about 400 years.

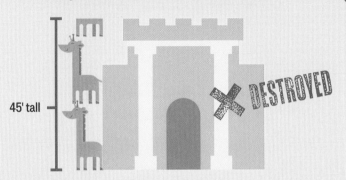

45' tall

DESTROYED

 After the Babylonians destroyed the temple, the **Ark of the Covenant disappeared from history.**

THE TOWER OF BABEL

 300 years after the Flood   Babylon (present-day Iraq)

Represented humanity's disobedience to God

DESTROYED

 We don't know what the Tower of Babel looked like, but it's generally accepted that it was a **ziggurat** in the Babylon area.

BIBLICAL : WORLD

Matthew 21:12-13

The temple during Jesus's ministry

DESTROYED

The Wailing Wall is the only part still standing

 After the Romans destroyed Herod's Temple, they may have used the **pieces of the temple to build the Colosseum.**

HEROD'S TEMPLE

 1st century BC   Jerusalem

Built as a gift for Nebuchadnezzar's wife, who was homesick for the mountains of her homeland

DESTROYED

75' tall

 An engineering feat! A large green mountain with ascending tiered gardens and all kinds of trees, shrubs, and vines.

THE HANGING GARDENS OF BABYLON

 600 BC   Babylon (present-day Iraq)

EPIC BATTLES OF THE BIBLE

LET'S GET READY TO CRUMBLE!

BATTLE OF JERICHO

JOSHUA 6

 ISRAELITES **VS** CANAANITES

 1406 BC 📍 JERICHO

BATTLE PLAN

DAY 1-6: God commanded Israel to march around the city of Jericho once a day without talking but with priests blowing trumpets and carrying the Ark.

DAY 7: March around the city 7 times and yell.

RESULT: THE WALL OF JERICHO CAME TUMBLING DOWN.

❗ The Wall of Jericho **actually had TWO walls.**

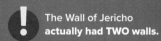 

INNER WALL — 46'

OUTER WALL — 20-26'

12-15'

BATTLE OF REPHIDIM

EXODUS 17:8-15

 ISRAELITES **VS** AMALEKITES

 1446 BC 📍 REPHIDIM

BATTLE PLAN

STAND TOGETHER: As long as Aaron and Hur held Moses's arms up, the battle went the Israelites' way.

RESULT: ISRAEL DEFEATED THE AMELEKITES

 There was once a man in India who held his arm up for more than **38 years.**

GIDEON'S 300

JUDGES 7–8:21

 ISRAELITES **VS** MIDIANITES

 1169 BC 📍 NEAR THE HILL OF MOREH

BATTLE PLAN

SIMPLIFY YOUR ARMY: Gideon started with an army of 32,000, but God whittled the army to only 300.

DON'T PANIC: The 300 Israelites went up against 135,000 Midianites.

OUTSMART THE ENEMY: Usually, only officers carried torches. But all 300 Israelites carried a torch, so the Midianites thought they were surrounded by thousands of men!

RESULT: THESE 300 MEN KILLED 105,000 MIDIANITES. THAT'S LIKE...

FOR EVERY **1 ISRAELITE** : THERE WERE **450 MIDIANITES** (400-450 KILLED BY **EACH** ISRAELITE)

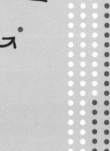

BATTLE OF MT. TABOR

JUDGES 4–5

 ISRAELITES VS CANAANITES

 1235 BC   📍 MT. TABOR

BATTLE PLAN

DON'T PANIC: 10,000 Israelites, led by Deborah and general Barak, fought against the Canaanites, led by Sisera, who had 900 iron chariots. Israel didn't have any, which put them at a huge disadvantage.

AN ACT OF GOD: God caused flooding, which immobilized Sisera's 900 chariots.

RESULT: ISRAEL DEFEATED THE CANAANITES. SISERA ESCAPED THE BATTLE BUT WAS KILLED BY A WOMAN NAMED JAEL.

❗ Chariots in that day were like tanks in our day. Imagine going up against 900 tanks when you had none!

FALL OF JERUSALEM

2 KINGS 25
2 CHRONICLES 36
JEREMIAH 52, DANIEL 1

 BABYLONIANS VS ISRAELITES

 587–586 BC   📍 JERUSALEM

BATTLE PLAN

SURVIVE: Jerusalem was under siege for about 2 years before they ran out of food.

RESULT: THE BABYLONIANS EVENTUALLY BROKE THROUGH THE WALL OF JERUSALEM. NEBUCHADNEZZAR BURNED THE TEMPLE AND CARRIED 4,200 ISRAELITES INTO CAPTIVITY.

REASON: This was God's judgment on Judah. Jeremiah wrote the book of Lamentations in response to the destruction of Jerusalem.

 Imagine being locked in your house for 2 years, surviving on **only the food you have right now!**

Two years' worth of food for one person is about **2,190 cheeseburgers.**

WINNING WITHOUT A FIGHT

2 CHRONICLES 20

 ISRAEL VS MOAB, AMMON, & EDOM

853 BC   📍 MT. SEIR

BATTLE PLAN

DON'T PANIC: The three armies united to attack Judah.

RESULT: GOD CAUSED THE THREE ARMIES TO TURN ON EACH OTHER! THE MEN OF JUDAH SIMPLY HAD TO CARRY OFF THE PLUNDER!

FALL OF BABYLON

DANIEL 5

 **PERSIANS** VS BABYLONIANS

539 BC   📍 BABYLON

BATTLE PLAN

STEAL: King Belshazzar, a descendant of Nebuchadnezzar, threw a big party and used the gold from God's temple in Jerusalem to pay for it.

BE WARNED: A giant hand appeared and wrote on the wall. Daniel interpreted the writing, explaining that the kingdom of Babylon would be ripped from Belshazzar that night.

BLINDSIDED: The Babylonians were distracted by the party. And though Babylon's walls were considered impenetrable at the time, the Persians diverted the Euphrates River (which ran under the city's walls). This allowed their soldiers to enter the city.

RESULT: BABYLON'S EMPIRE FELL, AND THE PERSIANS BECAME THE NEW RULERS.

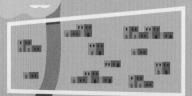

JUDGES

(*noun*) : In Hebrew, means "to put things right."

Judges were Israel's governors and deliverers from outside enemies. They served as leaders and settled disputes both internally and externally.

THE BOOK OF **JUDGES**:   **21** CHAPTERS   **618** VERSES   AUTHOR IS **UNKNOWN**

THE CYCLE OF SIN IN JUDGES

JUDGES 2

In those days there was no king in Israel.
Everyone did what was right
in his own eyes.

Judges 17:6 ESV

DELIVERANCE
Israel was
delivered

PEACE
Israel served
God

JUDGE
The Lord raised
up a judge

SIN
The Israelites
did evil

REPENTANCE
The Israelites cried
out for help

OPPRESSION
The Lord gave/sold them
to the enemy

THE GOOD, THE BAD-ISH, AND THE REALLY BAD
(Seriously, it's not good.)

OTHNIEL **EHUD** **SHAMGAR** **DEBORAH** **GIDEON** **TOLA** **JAIR** **JEPHTHAH** **IBZAN** **ELON** **ABDON** **SAMSON**

THE GOOD
DEBORAH

Judges 4–5 • Ruled 1250–1214, 36 years

 Prophetess and only woman judge

 Sat under a palm tree to hear people's problems

 Fought and beat King Jabin's army with Barak

THE BAD-ISH
GIDEON

Judges 6–8 • Ruled 1208–1170, 38 years

 Tore down the altar of Baal

 Defeated 135,000 Midianites with only 300 men

 Made his own gold into an ephod (a priestly garment) that became an object of worship

THE REALLY BAD
JEPHTHAH

Judges 11–12 • Ruled approx. 1100 BC, 6 years

 Was rejected by his tribe (Gilead) and led a band of dissidents

 Made a foolish vow to sacrifice his own daughter

 Dealt with war between Gilead and Ephraim

THE REALLY BAD
SAMSON

Judges 13–16 • Ruled 1081–1062, 19 years

 Given a superpower—like a superhero of super strength

 Broke his Nazarite vows and let Delilah know his secret

 Betrayed by Delilah, he was captured, blinded, and sentenced to hard labor.

 The book of Judges shows us that everyone fails—including the heroes and people in the Bible. **Jesus is the only real success story and one true Judge.**

$OLOMON

SON OF DAVID AND BATHSHEBA

THIRD KING OF ISRAEL

 1. Saul

2. David

3. Solomon

RULED 40 YEARS

Solomon humbly asked God for wisdom instead of riches when he became king. God granted him both wisdom and riches.

1 Kings 3:5-13

WHAT WAS HE WORTH?

$2.2 TRILLION

SOLOMON

FREE 2-DAY SHIPPING

$130 BILLION*

JEFF BEZOS

$88 BILLION*

BILL GATES

$72 BILLION*

MARK ZUCKERBERG

$64.5 BILLION

SCROOGE MCDUCK

$12.4 BILLION

TONY STARK

$9.2 BILLION

BRUCE WAYNE

*Plus or minus billions depending on the day and stock market. Bottom line, Solomon still wins!

HE ALONE COULD BUY...

 **31,429** FERARRIS

146,666 LOUISIANA PURCHASES

 **489,977,728,285** CHEESEBURGERS
or enough to give every person on the planet **64.5 cheeseburgers**

2,200 SOLOMON ISLANDS
Named after King Solomon by Alvaro De Mendana in 1568

WHAT DID SOLOMON DO WITH HIS RICHES?

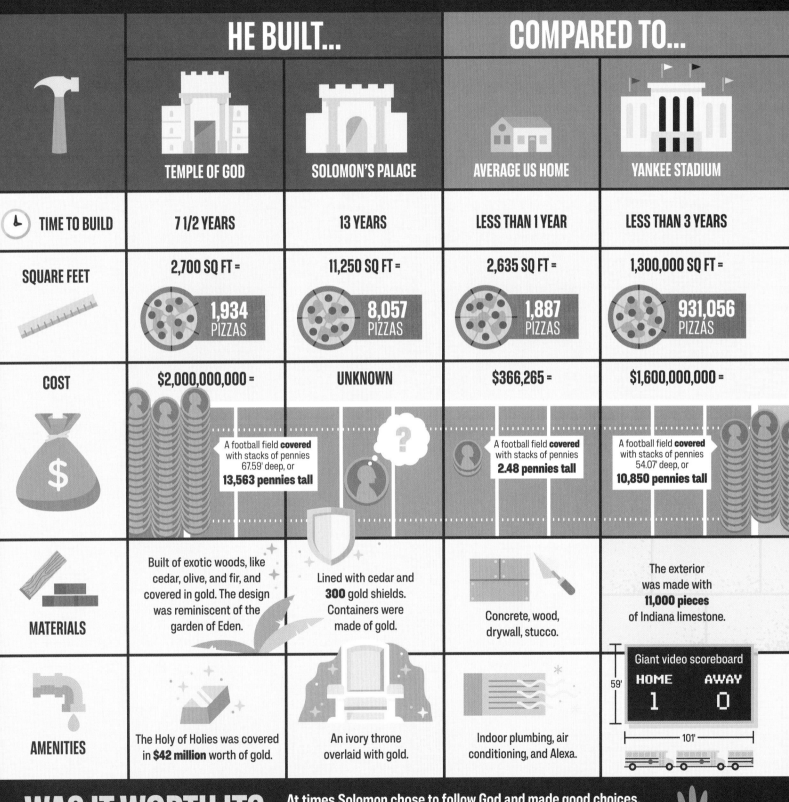

	HE BUILT...		COMPARED TO...	
	TEMPLE OF GOD	**SOLOMON'S PALACE**	**AVERAGE US HOME**	**YANKEE STADIUM**
TIME TO BUILD	7 1/2 YEARS	13 YEARS	LESS THAN 1 YEAR	LESS THAN 3 YEARS
SQUARE FEET	2,700 SQ FT = **1,934** PIZZAS	11,250 SQ FT = **8,057** PIZZAS	2,635 SQ FT = **1,887** PIZZAS	1,300,000 SQ FT = **931,056** PIZZAS
COST	$2,000,000,000 = A football field **covered** with stacks of pennies 67.59' deep, or **13,563 pennies tall**	UNKNOWN	$366,265 = A football field **covered** with stacks of pennies **2.48 pennies tall**	$1,600,000,000 = A football field **covered** with stacks of pennies 54.07' deep, or **10,850 pennies tall**
MATERIALS	Built of exotic woods, like cedar, olive, and fir, and covered in gold. The design was reminiscent of the garden of Eden.	Lined with cedar and **300** gold shields. Containers were made of gold.	Concrete, wood, drywall, stucco.	The exterior was made with **11,000 pieces** of Indiana limestone.
AMENITIES	The Holy of Holies was covered in **$42 million** worth of gold.	An ivory throne overlaid with gold.	Indoor plumbing, air conditioning, and Alexa.	Giant video scoreboard HOME **1** AWAY **0** 59' × 101'

WAS IT WORTH IT?

At times Solomon chose to follow God and made good choices, like humbly asking for wisdom instead of money. **But, despite God's gift of wisdom, he also made mistakes.** His sins caused problems for future generations of Israelites.

KINGS OF ISRAEL

The spiritual state of the **NATION** followed the spiritual state of its **LEADER**.

LEADER'S CHARACTER	**NATION'S** CHARACTER
 →	
→	

1030 BC	1010 BC	990 BC	970 BC	950 BC

Legend:

- Good
- Bad
- It's Complicated
- Assassinated
- Executed
- New Dynasty
- Direct Descendent
- Grandchild
- Mother
- Brother
- Prophet

THE UNITED KINGDOM

Israel at the height of its power and wealth **was united under a single king.**

 ISRAEL'S FIRST KING

 **ISRAEL'S MOST IMPORTANT KING**

SAUL

The prophet Samuel anointed Saul as king, turning Israel's **theocracy** into a **monarchy**.

THEOCRACY (*noun*) : government by **religious leaders** in the name of God or a god

MONARCHY (*noun*) : government by a **monarch** (a king or queen)

After disobeying God in a battle against the Amalekites, **Saul was rejected as king.**

He was killed by the Philistines at the Battle of Gilboa.

DAVID

Led Israel to its **political and religious high point.**

God promised that the Messiah would come from his family.
2 Samuel 7:12-16

Wrote most of the book of **Psalms.**

PSALMS

SOLOMON
↓ Son of David

The **wisest and richest man** who ever lived.

Built the temple and beautiful palaces.

Allowed his many wives to **lead him to idol worship.**

Wrote most of the book of **Proverbs, Ecclesiastes, and the Song of Solomon.**

PROVERBS
ECCLESIASTES
SONG OF SOLOMON

SAMUEL

NATHAN

THE DIVIDED KINGDOM

Because of Solomon's sin, the nation split into the **NORTHERN** and **SOUTHERN** kingdoms.

Jeroboam asked King Rehoboam (Solomon's son) for relief from Solomon's heavy taxes. **Rehoboam refused.**

So... The 10 northern tribes rejected him and made **JEROBOAM** their king.

And... The two southern tribes (Benjamin and Judah) followed King **REHOBOAM.**

ISRAEL

JUDAH

THE NORTHERN KINGDOM

THE SOUTHERN KINGDOM

910 BC   890 BC   870 BC   850 BC   830 BC

ISRAEL

JEROBOAM I
Tried to assassinate Solomon. He failed and fled to Egypt until Solomon died.

Introduced idol worship, which led to Israel's downfall.

BAASHA
Was a captain in Nadab's army.

Assassinated Nadab, beginning a string of violent successions, coups, and rebellions in Israel.

ZIMRI (7 DAYS)
Assassinated Elah but didn't have the support of the people, so he **burned down his own palace,** killing himself in the process.

TIBNI
CIVIL WAR

ELISHA

ELIJAH

ISRAEL'S WORST KING
AHAB
↓ Son of Omri

Ahab and Jezebel **killed many of God's prophets** and forced the entire nation to worship.

JORAM
Brother to Ahaziah

He and his nephew Ahaziah (king of Judah) were **killed by his captain, Jehu.**

He worshipped Baal.

JEHU
Assassinated the king of Israel and the king of Judah.

NADAB
↓ Son of Jeroboam I

ELAH
↓ Son of Baasha

OMRI

AHAZIAH
↓ Son of Ahab

CIVIL WAR

↓ Son of Rehoboam

ABIJAH

Killed by Jehu while visiting his uncle, King Joram of Israel.

↓ Son of Jehoram

AHAZIAH (1 YEAR)

JUDAH

REHOBOAM
↓ Son of Solomon

Eventually **abandoned God** and brought idol worship to the nation.

ASA
↓ Son of Abijah

Rid the land of idolatry.

JEHOSHAPHAT
↓ Son of Asa

Instead of continuing the war with Israel, **he made peace with them.**

He is often compared to Solomon because he **brought great prosperity to the kingdom.**

JEHORAM
↓ Son of Jehoshaphat

Married to Athaliah, daughter of Ahab and Jezebel

Extreme Baal worshipper. Killed his six brothers to secure the throne.

QUEEN ATHALIAH
Mother of Ahaziah

After her husband (Jehoram) and her son (Ahaziah) died, she **seized the throne by killing all the other royal males**—even her own grandsons!

JUDAH'S ONLY QUEEN

29

KINGS, QUEENS & PRESIDENTS, OH MY!

ENGLAND 66 Kings & Queens		
ISRAEL 43 Kings & Queens	414 Total Years	9.6 Years of Average Reign
UNITED STATES 44 Presidents	229 Total Years	5.2 Years of Average Term

790 BC   770 BC   750 BC   730 BC   710 BC

HOSEA

JONAH

AMOS

ZECHARIAH (6 MONTHS)
↓ Son of Jeroboam II

MENAHEM

PEKAHIAH
↓ Son of Menahem

He worshipped the golden calf.

CIVIL WAR

↓ Son of Jehoahaz
JEHOASH

JEHOAHAZ
↓ Son of Jehu

JEROBOAM II
↓ Son of Jehoash

SHALLUM (1 MONTH)
↓ Son of Jehoash

PEKAH

HOSHEA

He brought the nation great wealth, **but it didn't do them any good.** Assyria invaded and captured them 30 years later.

After murdering Zechariah, he **reigned just a month** before he was also murdered.

↓ Son of Joash
AMAZIAH

ISRAEL'S LONGEST-REIGNING KING

↓ Son of Uzziah
JOTHAM

JOASH

🙂 Grandson of Athaliah

UZZIAH (AKA AZARIAH)
↓ Son of Amaziah

AHAZ
↓ Son of Jotham

HEZEKIAH
↓ Son of Ahaz

Crowned king in a secret ceremony at 7 years old. He had been hidden for 6 years by a priest, protecting him from his grandmother, Queen Althaliah.

JUDAH'S YOUNGEST KING

Became king at 16.

A good military leader who reigned during **a time of great prosperity for Judah.**

He became proud and offered incense in the temple as a priest. In response, God struck him with a skin disease that deformed his face. Even so, **Uzziah is considered a king who did what was right in the Lord's eyes** (2 Kings 15:3).

Rejected Mosaic tradition (he shut the doors of the temple) and promoted Baal worship.

Sacrificed his own sons to Baal (2 Chronicles 28:3). He was not fit to be buried in the royal tombs.

Began radical religious reforms:

Destroyed idols and pagan altars.

Repaired the temple and opened its doors.

Invited both kingdoms of Israel to celebrate Passover in Jerusalem.

MICAH

ISAIAH

THE FALL, CAPTURE, AND EXILE OF THE KINGDOM

FALL OF THE NORTHERN KINGDOM
TO ASSYRIA IN 723 BC

Assyria deported Israel's leaders, **leaving the people kingless** and without their best and brightest.

THE FALL OF THE SOUTHERN KINGDOM
TO BABYLON IN 556 BC

From this line of fallen and flawed kings, **Jesus— the King of kings**—eventually came, a descendent of David and **the fulfillment of God's promise.**

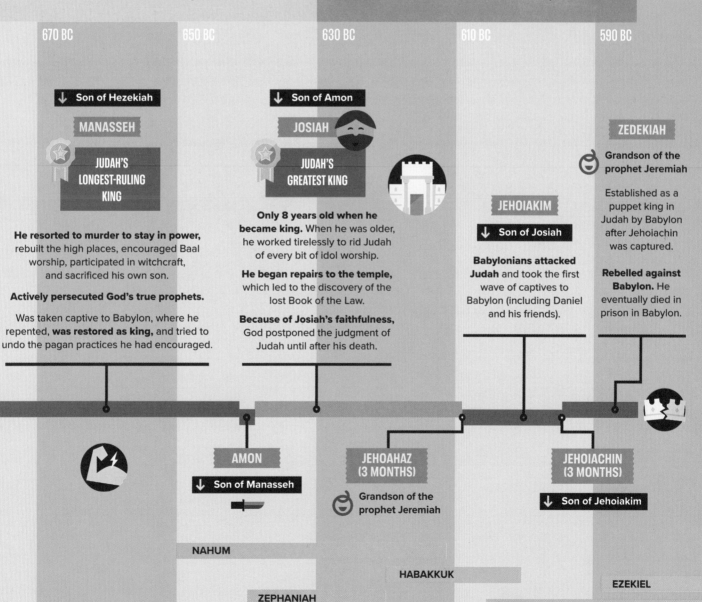

670 BC   650 BC   630 BC   610 BC   590 BC

↓ Son of Hezekiah

MANASSEH

JUDAH'S LONGEST-RULING KING

He resorted to murder to stay in power, rebuilt the high places, encouraged Baal worship, participated in witchcraft, and sacrificed his own son.

Actively persecuted God's true prophets.

Was taken captive to Babylon, where he repented, **was restored as king,** and tried to undo the pagan practices he had encouraged.

↓ Son of Amon

JOSIAH

JUDAH'S GREATEST KING

Only 8 years old when he became king. When he was older, he worked tirelessly to rid Judah of every bit of idol worship.

He began repairs to the temple, which led to the discovery of the lost Book of the Law.

Because of Josiah's faithfulness, God postponed the judgment of Judah until after his death.

ZEDEKIAH

Grandson of the prophet Jeremiah

Established as a puppet king in Judah by Babylon after Jehoiachin was captured.

Rebelled against Babylon. He eventually died in prison in Babylon.

JEHOIAKIM

↓ Son of Josiah

Babylonians attacked Judah and took the first wave of captives to Babylon (including Daniel and his friends).

AMON

↓ Son of Manasseh

JEHOAHAZ (3 MONTHS)

Grandson of the prophet Jeremiah

JEHOIACHIN (3 MONTHS)

↓ Son of Jehoiakim

NAHUM

HABAKKUK

ZEPHANIAH

EZEKIEL

DANIEL

JEREMIAH

EMPIRES OF MAN

King Nebuchadnezzar dreamed of a great statue that was made of **different materials, each representing a different empire.**

BABYLON
Head of Gold

King Nebuchadnezzar

The prophets **Ezekiel and Daniel prophesied** while in **Babylon.**

KING CYRUS

King Cyrus is mentioned by name **150 years before** he captured Babylon.
Isaiah 44:28–45:1

Defeated by King Cyrus in 539 BC.

PERSIA
Chest and Arms of Silver

King Cyrus
King Darius
Queen Esther

4 out of 10 people at the time lived under Persian rule.

The magi who visited Jesus were most likely priests from the Persian religion, Zoroastrianism.

Defeated by Alexander the Great in 331 BC.

GREECE
Abdomen & Thighs of Bronze

Alexander the Great

Introduced the **Olympics** and invented the **theater.**

Established a democracy in the 6th century BC.

Defeated by Rome in 146 BC.

ROME
Legs of Iron

Emperor Julius Ceasar

Early Christians were persecuted until the time of Constantine.
AD 306–AD 312

Built extensive roads making travel far easier than ever before.

Defeated by the Visigoths in AD 410 and again by the Vandals in AD 476.

DIVIDED KINGDOM
Feet of Iron and Clay

This kingdom is unstable because of its mixed and weak materials.

It possibly **represents our current divided world.**

HEAVEN

Where God lives
1 Kings 8:30

Sometimes called paradise or the third heaven
2 Corinthians 12:2-4

Where God's throne is
Isaiah 6:1

Cannot contain God
1 Kings 8:27

Angels surround God's throne
Revelation 4:8

Will not last forever
Revelation 21:1

OTHER WAYS HEAVEN IS USED IN THE BIBLE:

The celestial heaven
Psalm 8:3

The atmospheric heaven
Genesis 1:20 ESV

The kingdom of heaven
wherever God is ruling as King

Where Jesus lived before He came to earth as a man bringing with Him, the kingdom of heaven.

Matthew 4:17

After Jesus died and rose from the dead, **He returned to heaven** and is preparing the new heaven for His followers.

John 14:3

Right now, He rules in the hearts of believers on earth.

A BELIEVER'S SOUL will go to **heaven** to be with God.
2 Corinthians 5:8

WHAT HAPPENS WHEN PEOPLE DIE?

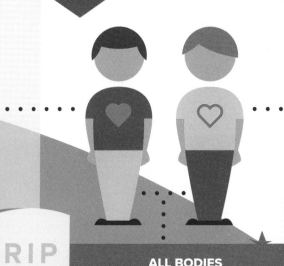

ALL BODIES will remain on the **earth** until the resurrection.
Philippians 3:21

RIP

HADES
Temporary location where unbelievers go after they die
Luke 16:23

A NON-BELIEVER'S SOUL will go to **Hades** to await final judgment.
Luke 16:23

THE KINGDOM OF GOD

Also known as
- **GOD'S KINGDOM** •
- **KINGDOM OF HEAVEN**•
- **NEW JERUSALEM** •

! John the Baptist was the first to preach about the arrival of God's kingdom.
Matthew 3:1-2

In King Nebuchadnezzar's dream, **a great rock struck the statue on its feet and destroyed the whole thing.** The rock then became a great mountain and filled the whole earth.

THE ROCK IS A SYMBOL OF THE KINGDOM OF HEAVEN.

Indestructible

Will bring an end to all earthly kingdoms and empires

Eternal

THE KINGDOM OF GOD IS LIKE...

Jesus never **defined** the kingdom but gave us pictures (parables) to **describe** it.

A MUSTARD SEED
Matthew 13:31-32

TREASURE HIDDEN IN A FIELD
Matthew 13:44

A VALUABLE PEARL
Matthew 13:45-46

LEAVEN
Luke 13:20-21

JESUS'S STORIES EMPHASIZE THAT GOD'S KINGDOM...

PRODUCES JOY

IS GROWING

COMING SOON

IS A FUTURE REALITY

GOD'S KINGDOM COMES TO EARTH

The seventh angel sounded his trumpet, and there were loud voices in heaven, which said: "The kingdom of the world has become the kingdom of our Lord and of his Messiah, and he will reign for ever and ever."
Revelation 11:15

33

ANGELS

(noun) : Mighty spirit beings who **serve God and aid His people**

FAMOUS ANGELS

MICHAEL
THE ARCHANGEL
Jude 9
Prince or ruler of angels
Daniel 10:13
Protector of the nation of Israel
Daniel 10:21

GABRIEL
THE MESSENGER OF GOD
Brought prophecies to Daniel
Daniel 8:1-16; 9:21-27
Announced the birth of John the Baptist
Luke 1:11-20
Announced Jesus's birth to Mary
Luke 1:26-38

CHERUBIM
Ezekiel 1:4-14

Extremely bright, like burnished bronze, torches, and lightening.

Four faces: a man, a lion, an ox, and an eagle

4 wings and 2 hands

2 legs and feet of a calf

Guarded the Garden of Eden and the Ark of the Covenant
Genesis 3:24; Exodus 25:17-22

ANGELS

Bright and beautiful, but also frightening
Daniel 8:16-17

Too many to count
Revelation 5:11

Wiser and stronger than men
2 Samuel 14:20

Spirits, though they can appear in bodies to humans
Hebrews 1:14

Created as higher than human beings, but not in God's image
Hebrews 2:6-7

SERAPHIM
Isaiah 6:1-3

Declare "Holy, Holy, Holy is the Lord God Almighty"

Wings to cover themselves from the bright glory of God

(noun, Hebrew) : burning ones

Two wings to fly

Surround the throne of God

HOW ANGELS INTERACT WITH HUMANS

Protect
Psalm 91:11

Encourage
Acts 27:23-25

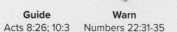
Guide
Acts 8:26; 10:3

Warn
Numbers 22:31-35

FACTS ABOUT ANGELS

Do not die
Luke 20:36

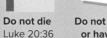
Do not get married or have children
Matthew 22:30

Aren't humans who died and went to heaven

There are no guardian angels

34

THE NEW HEAVEN AND NEW EARTH

Where God rules over the whole renewed universe
Isaiah 65:17-25

NO TEMPLE.
God dwells in the city
Revelation 21:22

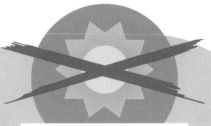

NO SUN.
God's glory will be the light
Revelation 21:23

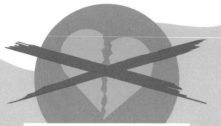

NO DEATH.
Or sorrow, crying or pain
Revelation 21:4

NO DOUBT.
We'll see Jesus face-to-face
1 Corinthians 13:12

WHEN JESUS RETURNS...ALL THE DEAD WILL RISE AND BE JUDGED...

THE NEW JERUSALEM

Believers will rise from the dead and receive new bodies.

Those whose names are not in the book of life will be thrown into the lake of fire along with Satan and his demons.

We will rest.
Hebrew 4:9-11

HALLELUJAH!
We will worship.
Revelation 19:1-4

We will serve God.
Matthew 25:14-30

We will feast.
Isaiah 25:6

We will enjoy God and His new creation.
Isaiah 65:17-19

HELL

a place of eternal torment for those who do not follow Jesus
Matthew 13:50

OTHER WAYS HELL IS DESCRIBED IN THE BIBLE:

The outer darkness
Mark 8:12

Unquenchable fire
Isaiah 66:24

The blazing furnace
Matthew 13:50

The lake of fire
Revelation 21:8

Satan is the not the ruler of Hell; it is a place of torment for him and his demons. Not a party!
Revelation 20:10

GEHENNA (*noun*, Greek) :

In the Old Testament, this was the name of **a valley outside Jerusalem** where people sacrificed to the god Molech.
2 Kings 16:3

Then in the New Testament, it was **the garbage dump for Jerusalem**. It became a symbol of the place where God would judge the wicked.
Matthew 10:28

VS DEMONS

(noun) : fallen angels who **rebelled against God** and were thrown from heaven

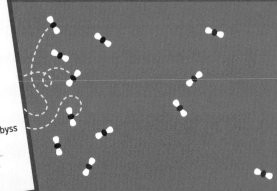

LUCIFER
THE FALLEN ANGEL

"Star of the morning"
Isaiah 14:12 NASB

Lived in heaven guarding God's throne
Ezekiel 28:14

Sinned and was thrown from heaven to the Abyss
Isaiah 14:15

Renamed Satan, meaning "adversary"
Matthew 4:10

SATAN

No horns or a pitchfork

Serpent
Revelation 12:9

Devil "Deceiver"
Matthew 4:1

Prince of the power of the air
Ephesians 2:2

Beelzebul "Lord of the flies"
Matthew 12:24

Disguised as an angel of light
2 Corinthians 11:14

Tempts believers to sin
1 Corinthians 7:5

Led a rebellion against God
Isaiah 14:13

Rules over the demons
Mark 3:22

Fights and accuses Christians
Ephesians 6:11-12

DEMONS

Intelligent, but they don't know everything

Originally in heaven but rebelled
Revelation 12:3-10

Can only be in one place at a time
Matthew 8:28-34

Spirits without bodies
Matthew 8:16

Powerful but no match for Jesus
Mark 5:1-20

THE DEFEAT OF SATAN AND THE DEMONS

Christians should be aware of Satan and his demons, **but we don't need to fear them because of Jesus.**

"He who is in you is greater than he who is in the world."
1 John 4:4 ESV

SEE WHAT HAPPENS NEXT

Satan will be defeated
Genesis 3:15

Jesus has power over demons
Mark 5:1-13

Satan is made powerless
Hebrews 2:14

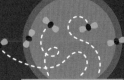
BAAL-ZEBUB
lord of the flies
2 Kings 1:1-6

CHEMOSH (MOLEK, MILCOM)
chief god of Moab
2 Kings 23:10

ASHTORETH
goddess of fertility
1 Kings 11:5

BAAL
god of strength, fertility and thunderstorms
1 Kings 16:31-32

DAGON
god of grain, possibly fish god
Judges 16:23

These gods had limits because each was one of many gods. **They were not self-sufficient or all-powerful.**

RA
god of the sun

HEQET
goddess of fertility

OLD TESTAMENT GODS

God consumed an offering with fire. Baal couldn't.
1 Kings 18:20-40

The presence of God knocked over the statue of Dagon.
1 Samuel 5:1-7

EGYPTIAN GODS

The Egyptians worshipped more than 50 gods. Each of the plagues in Exodus was aimed at humiliating one of the Egyptians gods.

INFAMOUS FALSE GODS

POSEIDON (NEPTUNE)
god of the sea

ZEUS (JUPITER)
chief God of the Greeks and Romans
Acts 14:12

HERMES (MERCURY)
messenger of the gods
Acts 14:12

ARTEMIS (DIANA)
goddess of fertility
Acts 19:24-28

HADES (PLUTO)
god of the underworld
Also see page 37

UNKNOWN GOD
Acts 17:16-24

GREEK & ROMAN GODS

The Greeks and Romans worshipped 12 main deities (the Olympians) along with countless other minor deities, demigods, and mythological figures. PLUS just in case they forgot one, they worshipped an "unknown god," which Paul says was really the one true God—they just didn't know it.

KING DARIUS OF PERSIA

Daniel 6:7

PHARAOH OF EGYPT

ROMAN EMPERORS

Idols are not real. They are representations of false gods made by humans out of wood, silver, and gold and **do not compare to the one true God.**

Isaiah 44:9-20

GOLDEN CALF

Representation of Yahweh
Exodus 20:4

HUMAN RULERS

Rulers were often worshipped as gods. But in the Bible, God constantly shows Himself as the King above all other kings.

GODS OF ISRAEL

The Israelites tried to create their own god (Exodus 32:1-6), but in doing so they violated the Second Commandment.

POLYTHEISM

(*noun*) : the belief in many gods

POLY = "MANY" | **THEISM = "GOD"**

IDOL

(*noun*) : an image of a deity used for worship

MONEY

POSESSIONS

RELATIONSHIPS

FAME

ACTIVITIES

MODERN-DAY IDOLS

We may not worship statues and burn sacrifices, but idolatry is still a problem today when we put these things before the one true God in our lives.

THE ONE TRUE GOD

Hear, O Israel; The LORD our God, the LORD is one.
Deuteronomy 6:4

Israel was different from all the other nations because **they believed in only one God**. They boldly claimed that God alone...

CREATED THE UNIVERSE

IS ALL-POWERFUL

IS WORTHY TO BE WORSHIPPED

MONOTHEISM

(*noun*) : the belief in only one God

MONO = "ONE" | **THEISM = "GOD"**

SAYS THERE ARE **NO OTHER** GODS
Isaiah 45:5

MEANS **NOTHING** (AND NO ONE) CAN COMPARE
Isaiah 40:25

AFFIRMS THE LORD RULES **OVER ALL** CREATION
Deuteronomy 10:14,17

DECLARES THERE IS ONLY **ONE WAY** TO BE SAVED
John 14:6

WHAT IS THE TRINITY?

EQUAL

The **FATHER**,
the **SON**,
and the **SPIRIT**
are all equally God.

Jesus has *"the whole fullness of deity."*
Colossians 2:9 ESV

DISTINCT

The Father, Son, and Spirit are not just three different names for the same person. They are **DIFFERENT FROM EACH OTHER.**

Jesus talks about the Father and the Spirit as different persons from Himself.
John 14:16

ONE

There are not three gods.
THERE IS ONLY ONE GOD.
"Hear, O Israel: The LORD our God, the LORD is one."
Deuteronomy 6:4

ONE GOD · THREE PERSONS

THE FATHER

DECIDES what to do

Decided to save us
Ephesians 1:3-6

THE SON

DOES what the Father says

Did the work needed to save us
Ephesians 1:7-12

THE SPIRIT

DISPLAYS what the Father and Son have done

Displays God's work by living inside believers
Ephesians 1:13-14

The word "TRINITY" never appears in the Bible. It was first used around AD 200, and for centuries, people have been trying to describe what it is.

Father   Son   Spirit

The Trinity is NOT like a shamrock

Each of the three leaves is not alone the whole clover. **The Trinity is only ONE God, not three.**

LEGEND HAS IT: St. Patrick used a shamrock to try to explain the Trinity to the pagan king of Ireland.

Tritheism (*noun*) : the belief that there are three gods, not one God

Father   Son   Spirit

The Trinity is NOT like the sun

Light and heat are products of the sun, not equal to the sun itself. **In the trinity, each person is EQUAL.**

LEGEND HAS IT: The real-life jolly old St. Nicholas gave Arius a whupping after Arius said Jesus was not equal to God the Father at the Council of Nicaea (AD 325).

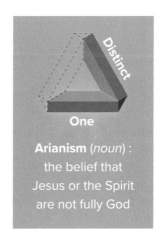

Arianism (*noun*) : the belief that Jesus or the Spirit are not fully God

Father   Son   Spirit

The Trinity is NOT like water

A water molecule cannot exist as water, ice, and steam all at once. **God is always three DISTINCT persons.**

Water is the most common substance on Earth, so it might be a better picture of God's omnipresence.

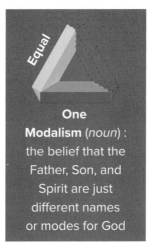

Modalism (*noun*) : the belief that the Father, Son, and Spirit are just different names or modes for God

JESUS:

WHY IT'S IMPORTANT JESUS IS **FULLY GOD**:

Only God is **perfect**,
only God has the **authority to forgive sins**,
only God can **conquer death**,
and only God can be **a true Savior**.

Jesus has TWO NATURES

TRULY & FULLY GOD

DIVINE
(*adj*) : relating to a supreme being

He has the same divine nature as God the Father and God the Spirit.

HUMAN
(*adj*) : having the nature of people

He has the same human nature as us.

yet He is only ONE PERSON.
Hebrews 1:3

His DIVINITY & HUMANITY are INSEPARABLE.

ARIANISM
The belief that Jesus was not *fully* God taught by Arius in the 4th century.

DOCETISM
The belief that Jesus only *seemed* human and that his humanity was an illusion.

Jesus is GOD the Son who took on a HUMAN body.

He is sovereign, ruling over everything
Matthew 11:27

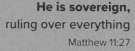

He is all-knowing, able to read the minds of those around him
Mark 2:8

He is all-powerful, able to control nature
Matthew 8:26-27

He is eternal, living before He became a human
John 8:58

He received worship from His followers
John 20:28

He is able to forgive sins
Mark 2:5-7

He is present everywhere
Matthew 28:20

THE GOD-MAN

WHY IT'S IMPORTANT JESUS IS FULLY MAN:

A righteous man was needed to be the substitute for all of mankind on the cross and undo what Adam had done.

Romans 5:12-21

TRULY & FULLY HUMAN

He wasn't **glamorous or notable**
Isaiah 53:3

He grew from a baby to an adult
Luke 2:40

He was **hungry and thirsty**
Matthew 4:2
John 19:28

He cried
John 11:35

He bled and died
John 19:30-34

He breathed
Luke 23:46

He was tired
Mark 4:38

Our Savior now knows what it's like to suffer as a human and can easily identify with our struggles.

Hebrews 4:14-16

WHEN JESUS WAS **HUNGRY**, HE COULD HAVE TURNED THE **STONES** TO **BREAD.**

But if He had, He would never have experienced human hunger.

Matthew 4:3-4

WHEN **JESUS** WAS ABOUT TO **DIE**, HE COULD HAVE CALLED DOWN **ANGELS** TO **STOP** HIS ARREST AND HIS CRUCIFIXION.

But if He had, He would have never experienced human death.

Matthew 26:53

GOOD NEWS!

THE FOUR GOSPELS

The four Gospels are the first four books of the New Testament, all recounting Jesus's crucifixion and resurrection. Each book has a unique style, purpose, and intended audience that **give a valuable, fully rounded portrait of Jesus and His journey!**

SYNOPTIC GOSPELS

(adj) : able to be seen together. **They're very similar** in story structure and wording.

 = **Audience and theme**

MATTHEW
TAX COLLECTOR

 AD 50-60

 To: Jews
JESUS IS KING!

 The Sermon on the Mount

 The only Gospel that mentions the magi (the "Wise Men" at Jesus's birth)

MARK
EVANGELIST

 AD 50-60

 To: Romans
JESUS IS SERVANT!

 Persecution is part of God's plan

 The shortest and most action-packed gospel!

Mark uses the Greek word *euthus* or "immediately" **40 times** in his Gospel— **12 times in one chapter alone!**

THE GOSPELS BY NUMBERS

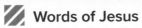

■ Words in Greek ▨ Words of Jesus

MATTHEW
60%   18,346

MARK
42%   11,304

LUKE
51%   19,482

JOHN
48%   15,635

UNIQUE MATERIAL

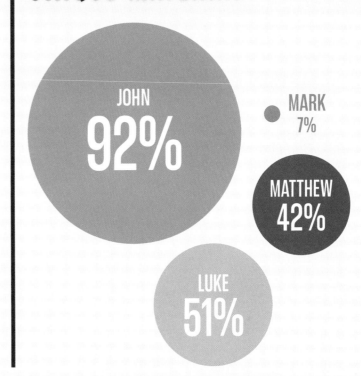

JOHN 92%

MARK 7%

MATTHEW 42%

LUKE 51%

 = **Key point**   = **Unique features**

JOHN isn't one of the synoptic gospels because the majority of the book's material **is different from the other three.**

LUKE
DOCTOR

 AD 60

✉ To: Greeks
JESUS IS SON OF MAN!

 The geography of Jesus's ministry

 The longest Gospel and New Testament book

 Luke is the New Testament's **most prolific author** by sheer volume of words!

JOHN
FISHERMAN

 AD 85-90

✉ To: Everyone
JESUS IS SON OF GOD!

 Jesus's death and resurrection bring Him glory

 The most uniquely written Gospel

Almost half covers the last week of Jesus's life!

THE RISE OF THE CHURCH

THE BEGINNING

JESUS founded the church.
Matthew 16:18-19

Jesus's followers received the **HOLY SPIRIT**.
Acts 2:1-13

The first Christians began to **SPREAD THE NEWS** of Jesus.

THE EARLY CHURCH

WHO?

The **12 APOSTLES** led the church.
Ephesians 2:20

ELDERS were pastors and overseers.
1 Timothy 3:1-7

DEACONS served the needs of the church.
1 Timothy 3:8-13

CHURCH FATHERS wrote letters to encourage the churches.

BISHOPS were appointed to supervise groups of churches within a region.

WHAT? ACTS 2:42-45

PREACHED from the Bible

TAUGHT from the Bible

ATE meals together

PRAYED together

SANG hymns and spiritual songs

GAVE to the poor

SHARED the Lord's Supper

WHERE?

THE TEMPLE in Jerusalem

SYNAGOGUES

CATACOMBS in Rome (underground burial caves)

PEOPLE'S HOMES Acts 2:46

WHEN?

SUNDAYS Acts 20:7

EARLY CHURCH GROWTH
Acts 11, 13, 16, 28

DURING ACTS
- Jerusalem, Judea, Samaria
- Antioch, Asia Minor
- Macedonia, Greece, Rome

AFTER ACTS
- Eastern Mediterranean • AD 100
- Roman empire • AD 400

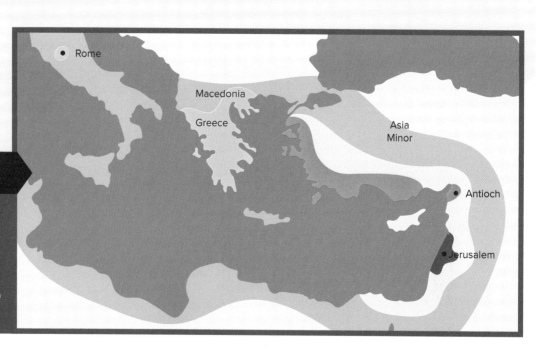

Rome

Macedonia

Greece

Asia Minor

Antioch

Jerusalem

PERSECUTION THEN

PERSECUTION TODAY

Jesus promised that the church would face persecution (Luke 21:17).

WHO WAS PERSECUTING THE EARLY CHURCH?

JEWISH LEADERS forced the church to expand beyond Jerusalem.
Acts 12

The **ROMAN EMPIRE** persecuted Christians as their popularity grew.

! Tradition says Peter and Paul were **executed under Emperor Nero's reign.**

215,000,000
Christians live in persecution.

That's more than the
208,846,892
population of Brazil

 ● ● ●
● ● ● **1 in 12**
● ● ●

Christians live where Christianity is illegal, forbidden, or punished.

! 1 Peter, 1 Thessalonians, 2 Thessalonians, Hebrews, and Revelation were written to **encourage Christians in persecution.**

THE CHURCH TODAY

4.8% **Russia**
104,750,000

2.6% **Germany**
56,540,000

11.2% **United States**
243,060,000

1 **North Korea**

2 Afghanistan

5 Pakistan

3.1% **China**
68,410,000

5% **Mexico**
107,910,000

4 **Sudan**

2.4% **Ethiopia**
52,070,000

4% **Philippines**
86,370,000

Nigeria **3.6%**
78,050,000

3 **Somalia**

 Most dangerous countries to follow Jesus in

● Highest percentage of global Christians

Brazil **8%**
173,300,000

DR Congo **2.9%**
63,210,000

! **Christians exist in every country in the world.** Christianity is growing the fastest in Sub-Saharan Africa, Latin America, and Asia

CHRISTIANITY IS SPREADING

CHRISTIANITY GREW RAPIDLY FROM 12 CHRISTIANS IN 30 AD TO 2,300,000,000 CHRISTIANS IN 2015

OF 16,600 PEOPLE GROUPS WORLDWIDE, 6,700 ARE **UNREACHED**
a population where less than 2% are true Christ-followers

THERE ARE ROUGHLY 419,500 **MISSIONARIES**
both Catholic and Protestant

WORLD RELIGIONS BY POPULATION

- Christians · 31.2%
- Muslims · 24.1%
- Unaffiliated · 16%
- Hindus · 15.1%
- Buddhists · 6.9%
- Folk religions · 5.7%
- Other · 0.8%
- Jews · 0.2%

WORLD POPULATION REACHED BY THE GOSPEL
- Reached · 58%
- Unreached · 42%

RATIO OF MISSIONARIES TO WORLD POPULATION

1 MISSIONARY : **17,878.43 PEOPLE**

THE FRUIT OF THE SPIRIT

The fruit of the Spirit is love, joy, peace, patience, kindness, goodness, faithfulness, gentleness and self-control.
Galatians 5:22-23

LOVE

Affection, goodwill.

Matthew 22:39

JOY

A feeling of happiness or gladness.

Luke 2:10

PEACE

A state or feeling of calm.

Philippians 4:7

PATIENCE

The ability to accept delay or hardship.

Proverbs 25:15

IDOLATRY

Worship of idols or false gods.

(See Pages 40-41 for more!)

ENVY

Feeling discontented or resentful about another person or their possessions.

1 Samuel 18:8-9

Alone, we can't resist the flesh or sin in our lives. But by resting in the promises of God and walking with the Holy Spirit, we can weed out that sin. The result—fruit!

"Remain in me, as I also remain in you. **No branch can bear fruit by itself; it must remain in the vine.** Neither can you bear fruit unless you remain in me. **I am the vine; you are the branches.** If you remain in me and I in you, you will bear much fruit; apart from me you can do nothing."

John 15:4-5

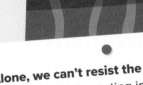

FITS OF RAGE

Outbursts of anger.

Ephesians 4:26

KINDNESS

Quality of being friendly, good, generous.

Zechariah 7:9

GENTLENESS

Quality of being kind, fair, mild.

Ephesians 4:2

SELF-CONTROL

The ability to control oneself, especially in a difficult situation.

Matthew 4:1-11

GOODNESS

Quality of being good or upright.

3 John 1:11

FAITHFULNESS

Quality of believing truth and trusting.

Genesis 12:1,4

DRUNKENNESS

Being intoxicated or out of control.

Ephesians 5:18

SELFISH AMBITION

Doing something for your own personal gain at the expense of others.

Mark 10:35-45

HATRED

A strong dislike for someone to the point of hoping something bad will happen to that person.

1 John 4:20

WITCHCRAFT

The practice of magic or believing someone other than God can do wonderful things.

1 Samuel 28

DISCORD

A disagreement between people or a lack of harmony.

Titus 3:10

THE WORKS OF THE FLESH

The flesh desires what is contrary to the Spirit, and the Spirit what is contrary to the flesh.

Galatians 5:17

FANTASTIC ANIMALS

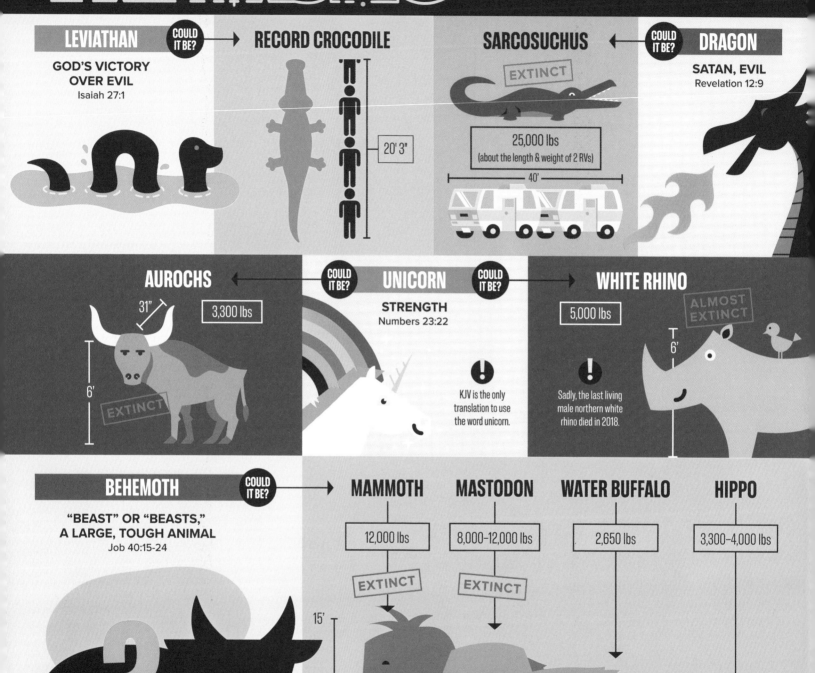

LEVIATHAN — COULD IT BE? → **RECORD CROCODILE**

GOD'S VICTORY
OVER EVIL
Isaiah 27:1

20' 3"

SARCOSUCHUS ← COULD IT BE? — **DRAGON**

EXTINCT

25,000 lbs
(about the length & weight of 2 RVs)

40'

SATAN, EVIL
Revelation 12:9

AUROCHS ← COULD IT BE? — **UNICORN** — COULD IT BE? → **WHITE RHINO**

31"

3,300 lbs

6'

EXTINCT

STRENGTH
Numbers 23:22

! KJV is the only translation to use the word unicorn.

5,000 lbs

ALMOST EXTINCT

6'

! Sadly, the last living male northern white rhino died in 2018.

BEHEMOTH — COULD IT BE? → **MAMMOTH**   **MASTODON**   **WATER BUFFALO**   **HIPPO**

"BEAST" OR "BEASTS,"
A LARGE, TOUGH ANIMAL
Job 40:15-24

?

12,000 lbs

EXTINCT

8,000–12,000 lbs

EXTINCT

2,650 lbs

3,300–4,000 lbs

15'

10'

5'

OF THE BIBLE

PIG

PAGANISM, UNCLEANNESS, WICKEDNESS
Luke 8:33

Pigs can live up to 27 years.

700 LBS

500 LBS

BEAR

FEROCIOUS NATURE, FEAR
Lamentations 3:10

David killed a bear.

500 LBS

27 MPH

DONKEY

WEALTH, INFLUENCE

Jesus rode into Jerusalem on a donkey to fulfill a prophecy.
Matthew 25:21

40 MPH

50 MPH

HORSE
STRENGTH, POINTING TO GOD'S GREATER STRENGTH • Psalm 20:7

CAMEL
PATIENCE, TOLERANCE, WEALTH, AND ENDURANCE • Isaiah 60:6

can carry up to 1,000 lbs

LION
STRENGTH, VICTORY, BOLDNESS, WICKEDNESS, AND THE MESSIAH • 1 Peter 5:8

Samson, David, and Benaiah all killed a lion.

RANGE OF VISION

160-210°	360°	360°	320-340°	270°
HUMAN	LAMB	SHEEP	GOAT	OWL

can be taught to answer to their name when called

HUMAN
Genesis 1:26

LAMB
INNOCENT, DEFENSELESS, AN IDEAL KINGDOM, JESUS
1 Peter 1:19

SHEEP
PEOPLE WITHOUT LEADERSHIP OR UNITY, HUMAN SIN, INNOCENCE, HELPLESSNESS
Matthew 10:16

GOAT
UNBELIEF AND IDOL WORSHIP OR SOMETIMES STRENGTH AND REGALITY
Matthew 25:32

OWL
JUDGMENT, DESOLATION, SADNESS OR MISERY
Micah 1:8

The blood of the lambs on doorposts protected the Israelites from the 10th plague.

Owls are nocturnal – living in the darkness

SNAKE
WICKED, PERSECUTOR, THE ENEMY, SATAN • Genesis 3:1

Snakes don't have eyelids, they swallow their food whole, and they smell with their tongue.

FISH

Early Christian churches used the Greek word for fish (**icthus**) to represent Jesus.

I	*iesous*	= **Jesus**
X	*christos*	= **Anointed**
Θ	*theou*	= **God**
Y	*huios*	= **Son**
Σ	*soter*	= **Savior**

INDEX

Explore Bible Infographics
on the WORLD WIDE WEB*

*WEIRD WAY OF SAYING THE INTERNET**

**ASK YOUR PARENTS BEFORE GOING ONLINE

BibleInfographics.com

Facebook: @bibleinfographicsforkids